23rd Psalm

By Donald Curtis

INTERPRETATION *and* MEDITATIONS

DEVORSS *Publications*

MW01132913

The Lord Is My Shepherd

1 **THE LORD IS ONE** The Lord is our recognition of the Unity of all Life. The Lord is our ruling consciousness — that which we really are. The closer we come to complete understanding, the more power is released, as the Lord flows unobstructedly through us. The Lord is the Law. The completeness of the Law is available to each of us at all times. Unlimited power is at our disposal. We limit it or release it by our thoughts and our beliefs. Thus, "each man is a law unto himself"; but everpresent within us, awaiting release, is the full power of the One Law — the Lord of Life, which knows nothing of anything other than the true Nature of God.

The Lord is the Law. It is by nature a willing servant, but it assumes the role of a cruel master when our false beliefs and negative attitudes impose limitations upon its free activity. When this happens, we are in bondage of our own making and can be freed only by developing an awareness and sense of Unity with the Lord. This is the Law of Growth. "Ignorance of the Law is no excuse"; but even the most trying and painful experiences are valuable, because they teach us lessons and bring us into focus with true Being — with the Lord, the Law of Life.

I am not alone. "Hear, O Israel: the Lord our God, the Lord is One." I am aware of the Unity of all Life and all experience. I know there are more things in heaven and in earth than are dreamt of in my philosophy. I am a part of the great unfoldment of the Law. I cooperate with Life as the Lord acts through me. "The Lord is my light and my salvation; whom shall I fear? The Lord is the strength of my Life; of whom shall I be afraid?" I am filled with renewed confidence and expectancy today. My purpose is clear. I live to sustain the continuity of the right action of the Law. The day of the Lord is at hand. I make way for the coming of the Lord in my own heart. And so it is.

The Lord Is My Shepherd

2 **THE LORD IS MY SHEPHERD** We are guided and protected by the perfect working of the Law. There are no deviations from its balanced function and operation. There is no escape from every "jot and tittle of the Law." "As a man thinketh in his heart, so is he." "Whatsoever man soweth, that shall he also reap." The Lord shepherds us with a perfect system of discipline which teaches us to obey the Law.

We can have anything we desire if we love the Lord with all our hearts, with all our souls, and with all our minds. We can also have anything we desire even if we love "mammon" instead of God, but we will have to pay the penalty for the immature understanding which leads us to worship false gods. "We are not punished for our sins; we are punished by them."

In this way does the Lord shepherd us. Personal discipline is inherent in the Law; we are given complete freedom of choice. We can either cooperate by maintaining a sense of closeness and unity with the Shepherd, or we can strike out on our own and disregard Him in an attempt to do it all ourselves. When the false ego gets in the way, we get lost and cry for help. When the help arrives, as it always does, it is the action of the "Good Shepherd"—the Lord—bringing the lost sheep back into the fold.

I am constantly under the protection of the Lord, who is my shepherd. I cannot stray; I cannot be lost. "If I ascend up into heaven thou art there. If I make my bed in hell, behold thou art there." The Lord gives me purpose and direction, which keep me on the right path. "Strait is the gate and narrow is the way," but I enter therein. I stay in the fold of love, growth, and service. The Lord within me leads me always to express that which is of and for the greatest good. I love the Lord who is my Good Shepherd. And so it is.

I Shall Not Want

3 **I SHALL NEVER WANT** When we want for anything, it is because we have broken our connection with God. We become separated from the One Source, forgetting that "all things that the Father hath are mine." When this happens, the Good Shepherd helps us by leaving us alone to help ourselves. We are forced to develop resourcefulness and fulfillment by strengthening our Faith to the point where we really believe that "Before they call, I will answer; and while they are yet speaking, I will hear." It is usually by experience that we must learn to "Fear not, little flock; for it is your Father's good pleasure to give you the kingdom."

What could we possibly want if we believe in the Lord and do good? God is all in all. He is the source of all supply. A sustained consciousness of the Presence of God is the answer to every need. "Ask, and it shall be given unto you; seek, and ye shall find; knock and it shall be opened unto you." We don't pay enough attention to the promises which the Lord has made to us. We need to pray believing that we have already received. "According to your Faith be it unto you." As our Faith is strengthened, we come to realize that we cannot be separated from our good. What could we possibly want when the Lord has already seen to it that we have everything?

I am immersed in the abundance of fulfilled experience today. God works through me to express ever and ever larger patterns of Himself. Freely I have received the gift of Divine Love, and freely I give it place in my life. I prove the Lord herewith and believe Him as He says, "I will open the windows of heaven, and pour you out a blessing, that there shall not be room enough to receive it." I know that the Lord has given me "good measure, pressed down and shaken together, and running over." As I love God, He loves me and gives me all the Good which I deserve. The three of us cannot be separated. We are one. And so it is.

He Maketh Me to Lie Down in Green Pastures

4 **GOD COM-**
MANDS ME
There is That within each of us which literally makes us grow into ever greater expressions of Life. This Indwelling Presence is our own Higher Self—the Lord of our being. It is God individualized within us, the most compelling influence in our lives. To deny Its promptings is to betray our Lord and to slip backward on the ladder of progress. To affirm Its Presence and Power is to clear the way for the expression of abundant Life. The Lord within us is what we really are—the perfect pattern for all of our aspirations—the spiritual matrix for all manifestation.

The Lord is the Absolute Ruler of our destiny. His commands keep us constantly working toward self-conquest so that His Will may work through us. We avail ourselves of His Will, Wisdom, and Love when we learn to say and mean, "Father, not my will, but thine be done." When we act from the reference point of the Real Self, we are freed from the tyranny of physical, emotional, and mental desires, and we express the Power and the Presence of the Lord in everything we do.

"The Father worketh hitherto and I work." I seek no way other than to do the Will of the Lord. I know that He makes my life, and through His Law I am made to learn and grow from experience. I give thanks for all of Life's experiences today. I give thanks for the action of Infinite Mind in my world of affairs and activities. I give thanks for the compulsion to constantly improve myself. I give thanks for the rewards which come from following in His steps. I love the Way of the Lord. I love Life. I love all creatures here below. Love is the fulfilling of the Law—the only Power in the Universe. Love is the Lord in action. I love to live and work in the service of the Lord and my fellow beings today and forever. And so it is.

He Maketh Me to Lie Down in Green Pastures

5 **I AM IN PEACEFUL REPOSE**

Inner peace is the starting point for any personal creative activity. Emotional and mental turbulence can manifest only as confusion and destruction in our bodies and in our world. Action must always be from within outward. We must learn always to act from the peace within ourselves—the Kingdom of Heaven—and not to react to the appearances around us—the world. Jesus said, "In the world you shall have tribulation: but be of good cheer; I have overcome the world," affirming that That which is within us is greater than that which is in the world.

Universal Truth is: "As it is above, so it is below." At the individual level, Truth is expressed: "As a man thinketh in his heart, so is he." We must learn to "keep thy heart with all diligence; for out of it are the issues of Life." We become perfect even as our Father in Heaven is perfect when we learn to "seek ye first the kingdom of God, and his righteousness; and all these things shall be added unto you." We find that the door to the Kingdom of inner peace is opened as we follow the instruction of Paul: "Whatsoever things are true, whatsoever things are honest, whatsoever things are just, whatsoever things are pure, whatsoever things are lovely, whatsoever things are of good report; if there be any virtue, and if there be any praise, think on these things."

I repose in perfect peace today. I walk in the peaceful garden of the Lord. I am calmed and strengthened by constant contact with His Presence. The peacefulness of Loving Spirit flows through my consciousness. My ordered mind deals thoroughly and confidently with a continuous procession of noble thoughts and ideas. My emotions cooperate and give power and significance to "visitors from on high" as they are woven into the fabric of my life. I know that God has had His arm around me for a long time; He is never going to take it away. Confidently and peacefully, I walk forward with my hand in His—releasing all human concerns into His keeping as I live in the Kingdom of perfect inner peace. And so it is.

He Maketh Me to Lie Down in Green Pastures

6   **I LIE DOWN IN GREEN PASTURES**
Receptivity and not activity is the key to fulfillment. We do not need to constantly strive, struggle, and labor by the sweat of our brow. Accomplishment results first from what we know and are, and only secondarily from what we do. We are strengthened by grazing in the green pastures of the Spirit, so that we may then go forward and do our outer work in the world. The green pastures are the place of all abundance. They are the originating point of the One Source. We find all that we need—inspiration, guidance, faith, love, substance, health, fulfillment—in the green pastures.

How important it is that we lie down in these verdant spiritual pastures! The green pastures are the substance of Eternal Life. They provide the food of the Spirit. They are "our dwelling place in all generations." The green pastures are the place of prayer, the area of unification between God and His creation. They are the habitation of Spirit—the destination of the Soul. The green pastures are the area and the evidence of perfect demonstration. They are the Kingdom of Heaven.

My heart and my mind rest their labors today. I "let this mind be in me, which was also in Christ Jesus" by thinking from the conviction of Good which comes when my thoughts marry my emotions. I go with this spiritual mind of the "new man" into the habitation of peace. I lie down in green pastures. I bathe in the Allness of Spirit. I bask in the radiance of perfect expression. I embrace the action of abundance. I rest from outer activity as I turn my thoughts inward to "the secret place of the most High." How peaceful is my repose as the action of Spirit is released through me! I release all worries and outer concerns as I build my temple in the abundant fields of the green pastures. I lay down my cares, and my personal will lies enfolded in the Will of the Lord. As I forgive myself my sins, I "arise, take up my bed and walk," and make it anew amid the green pastures. And so it is.

He Leadeth Me Beside the Still Waters

7 GOD LEADS ME

We all have a bright, shining star to follow. This is the "star of the East"—spiritual knowing—which lights the path to the place where the Christ Consciousness is born within our own hearts. Our sole purpose in Life is to follow this Star in all ways and in all things. This Star is the visible evidence of the Lord. Its aspects are inspiration, intuition, and understanding. This Star is the highest awareness of our own being and the means by which God leads us. We all follow what we know to be true. "God is a Spirit; and they that worship Him must worship Him in Spirit and in Truth."

Life is for the purpose of developing the best means for accomplishing the greatest good. This means that we must discover the reality of God within ourselves. Our subjective knowing of this Truth leads us into ever and ever greater expressions of Good, until we consciously recognize that it is the Lord—the Law of Life—which has been leading us all the time. Once knowing this, without hesitation we give all that we have to the poor and follow Him. We can follow Him with complete Faith, because He can only lead us home—to the recognition of the Real Self.

God may not tell me which path to choose, but
He will never let me take the wrong one. Today
I move forward in confidence and dedication.
I know that "He leadeth me." First, I talk every-
thing over with God in prayer, and then I go
"about my Father's business." I know that what
I am doing is the most important thing in the
world for me at this moment, so I do it well.
After Prayer, I do gladly what I am led to do,
knowing that it is the right thing for me to do at
this time. As I learn to follow Him who leadeth
me, I am led out of darkness into light, from
ignorance into enlightenment, and from death
into immortality. As I become a doer of the
Word, I learn to lead others into paths of right
thinking and right living. I am thankful for the
love and guidance of the Supreme Leader today.
And so it is.

He Leadeth Me Beside the Still Waters

8 **I AM BESIDE THE STILL WATERS**

In the Bible, "water" always refers to some aspect of the mental and spiritual potential within the individual. The "still waters" are the quiet places of the mind where God resides. When we are "beside the still waters" we are next to the One Power—the only Power there is. Emerson says, "God is That which peoples the lonely places"—where peace, quiet, and stillness are supreme. In this place is the resting place of "the pearl of great price." "It is a consummation devoutly to be wished." Within the still waters are the means for attainment, accomplishment, and fulfillment.

As the Lord leads "beside the still waters," He takes us inside ourselves. Here we are free from the stormy and turbulent waters of worldly concern and outer activity. The still waters are beyond purely material, emotional, and mental concerns. They are the waters of the Spirit. They are always peaceful and untroubled. As we bathe in these waters and drink of them, we are filled with the qualities of Spirit, and these automatically make all of our waters —our thoughts, feelings, and activities—"still waters."

Peace—"be still and know that I am God." I follow the Spirit as I go into the quiet place within. God hears me there, because I know what I am saying. I speak from the heart. From the smooth surface of the still waters, peace, beauty, and good are reflected into my world. I look into the depths and discover the Secret of Life. In my still waters I am free from fear. Faith dwells there. I am free from trouble. Peace dwells there. I am free from imperfection. Wholeness dwells there. I am free from limitation. Abundance dwells there. I am free from bondage. Freedom dwells there. I am free from ignorance. Enlightenment, wisdom, and understanding dwell there.

I am free of my little self. God dwells there. I am not alone. Love is in action there, fulfilling the Law, and making all things new. And so it is.

He Restoreth My Soul

9 **MY SOUL IS RESTORED**
Each of us has a soul. We can never lose it, so the instruction here is not that our soul is given back to us, but that prayer and meditation will restore it to its natural state—one of contact with, and reflection of, the true Inner Individuality which is the Lord. An interesting remark was made by Don Blanding when someone reacted to his statement of his spiritual convictions by exclaiming, "Oh dear, I certainly hope that you are not a lost soul!"

"My dear sir, do you believe that God is all in all?" Don asked.

"Of course I do," was the reply.

"Then would you please tell me where I would go to get lost?"

Our souls are our personal responsibility. They represent what we do with the gift of Sonship which God has given us. We can build the soul into a stately mansion, or we can neglect it and starve it until it seems to be a lost cause. But it is never lost. It can always be restored when we pay some attention to its upkeep and growth. The elixir of restoration is completely spiritual and demands our attention upon the good, the true, and the beautiful, so that it may be released to flow through us. Muhammad said, "If I had two coats, I would sell one and buy white hyacinths for my soul." Jesus instructed the rich young man, "Give all that you have to the poor and follow me," thereby showing us that abundant worldly possessions are of no avail unless we are in the service of the Lord within.

I weave the seamless robe of my soul today as I dedicate my life to learning the lessons which the Lord has given me to learn. I express grace in living in all relationships. I know peace in mind and heart. I love all people. I blend knowledge and experience into wisdom and understanding. Gentleness characterizes my every word and deed. The words of my mouth and the meditations of my heart express purity. I experience the sweet release of renunciation as I give up all worry, doubt, and resentment. I am no longer tempted by the illusion of outside appearance. I drink from the sweet waters of Life within. I discipline my mind, my emotions, and my actions to follow through on the journey toward Truth and Reality. I cast the burden of my personality upon the Lord and build my soul in His image and likeness. And so it is.

He Leadeth Me in the Paths of Righteousness for His Name's Sake

10

I FOLLOW THE PATHS OF RIGHTEOUSNESS

There are no other paths. There are no shortcuts. We can't get something for nothing. We think we can, but this is just judging by appearances. The Law tells us to "judge righteous judgment" — to think from the premise of Truth, not to attempt conclusions based upon false premises. God alone is completely Good, therefore his existence and indwelling Reality is the only valid premise. All knowledge and all experience start from here. The paths of righteousness are the means by which we deductively reason that "God is, therefore I am."

The Buddha, in the "Noble Eight-Fold Path," teaches us that we must walk in Right Comprehension, Right Resolution, Right Speech, Right Conduct, Right Living, Right Effort, Right Concentration, and Right Meditation, if we are to live the Way of the Lord. These eight branches of the One Path lead the way to true righteousness, or right living. Righteousness is not to be confused with "self-righteousness," which is merely justifying our own personal opinions and habits no matter how inadequate they may be. When we aspire to true righteousness, we must be willing to change completely if necessary. When we establish right attitudes within, our lives reflect the inner righteousness of the Spirit, and we experience right action.

I judge not according to the appearance, but I endeavor to judge righteous judgment. I look for the best in everything and in everybody. I know that perfection dwells at the center of every person. We are all created in the image and likeness of the One Perfection. This is my Lord—my "dwelling place in all generations." I know intuitively that I am part of this Inner Reality, which is the criterion of all righteousness. I conduct myself righteously by learning to think rightly about everything in life. I respond rightly to all people because I love them. My joyful, expectant, and thankful attitudes toward life attract beauty and abundance into my experience. I am always in my right place at the right time. I determine to be the right kind of person. I act only from the highest level of consciousness of which I am capable. In all that I do, I make a sincere effort to walk uprightly in the Way of the Lord. And so it is.

He Leadeth Me in the Paths of Righteousness for His Name's Sake

11 **I PRAY IN HIS NAME** There is no limit to what we can be and do when we conduct this business of Life in His Name. The great statements of the Twenty-Third Psalm describe the state of our true being when we maintain this sense of Oneness with the Lord—the Law of Life. Our business in Life is to "hallow the name" of the Lord. This is the basic work in personal consciousness set forth by Jesus in the Lord's Prayer, which is really an amplification of the Twenty-Third Psalm. Jesus said, "After this manner therefore pray ye" and illustrated the same steps of unfolding realization which are given in this older prayer. A psalm is a song to God, and it expresses the soaring consciousness of ideally realized personal life.

The "Lord" is everyone's generic surname. We are all One with the Lord. He is constant and complete, but we are incomplete in our expression of Him. When we give lesser names to the Lord, that is what He becomes to us. When we reverse our thought, all limitation disappears as we do all things "for His Name's sake,"— that is, according to the Will of the greatest good—for the best interest of everyone concerned. We cannot escape our true nature. When we worship false gods and make graven images, we are taking the Name of the Lord in vain. When we name Him truly, we shall "see Him as He is" and we then become the recipients of the blessings described in this Psalm.

Pat Rogers

335 - 5158

*The Way of the Lord is my way all the days of
my life. I neither know nor desire any other way.
I do all things in His Name. I declare all things
in Christ which strengtheneth me. I cast my
burden upon the Lord and He sustains me.
What I name a thing, that is what it is—to me.
I forget all lesser names today, and I expand my
consciousness to call everything by His Name. I
am man, but also God in man—therefore, I am
one with the Lord. The Lord is my greater part
—my real Self. He is my life's partner—my
heart's companion. I place all of my property
and conduct all of my business in His Name. I
cannot breathe, move, nor live without Him. He
creates, maintains, and sustains me. I am One
with the Lord today. And so it is.*

Yea, though I Walk through the Valley of the Shadow of Death—

12   **GOD WALKS WITH ME**

The only feet God has to walk with are our feet. The only steps He can take through us are the steps which we first take for ourselves, with His guidance. The power of decision is ours; we initiate action by our decisions in the use of the thoughts and ideas which come to us from the Infinite Mind. Sometimes we think we do it all ourselves, but we can only accomplish anything when we do it in cooperation with the One Power. God creates; man discovers. God is Being; we are becoming.

When we were babies taking our first steps, a loving parent took our hand and walked beside us until we gained strength, balance, direction, and confidence. Even after we could navigate without the sustaining paternal hand, we always felt better when we knew it was there if we needed it. Thus we are with God. He is always the loving Father, and we are always His children, no matter how mighty and self-sufficient we think ourselves. When we forget the gentle, sustaining Presence which walks beside us and guides our steps, we fall down, and can only rise again with His help.

It is good to think of the Lord as our Higher Self. We can never be separated from Him. Whether we know it or not, He is our constant companion and teacher—"an ever-present help" in all situations. This is the real message of the Twenty-Third Psalm.

*Oh He walks with me, and He talks with me,
and He tells me that I am His own.*

*Speak to Him, thou, for He hears,
And Spirit with Spirit can meet.
Closer is He than breathing,
And nearer than hands or feet.*

*My steps are determined by Him who walks
beside me always. I trust in the Lord with all my
might and He directs my paths. I am never
alone. The Lord is my constant companion. He
makes me a king in my world by giving me
authority to share His power. Wonderful paths
of abundant experience open before me today as
I walk with the Lord in the way of service. I
may move slowly, but with His Presence guiding
and strengthening me, I move steadily onward
and upward. I am never afraid. He gives me
faith in the Law of justice and the purpose of
Life. I walk with Him, "spreading the Gospel
through all of Galilee." And so it is.*

Yea, though I Walk through the Valley of the Shadow of Death—

13 THERE IS NO DEATH

Death is an appearance, not a reality, hence the psalmist speaks of "the valley of the *shadow* of death." The shadow is never the real thing, merely the projection. If we believe in death, our thought casts a distorted shadow over our lives and we are forced to walk through the valley—the low place in consciousness. The false belief in death can be dissolved only by a true concept of Life. Life inhabits the mountains—the high places of the Soul, where Spirit dwells. The level of our thought determines the elevation of our experience. There are no shadows cast when we walk on the mountaintops. Only the Real exists in the rarified atmosphere of Spirit.

The spiritually enlightened agree that worldly living is really the state of death, and that true life comes when we free the Spirit from the fetters of material concern. We die daily in the world, but we live eternally in the Kingdom of Spirit. Our "kingdom is not of this world"—death. Ours is the "Kingdom of Heaven" —Life.

A living soul cannot die. I live eternally. There was never a time when I was not; there will never be a time when I will cease to be. Knowing this, there is no need for me to walk in the low, shadowy places. I take the high road in all of my travels, and as I believe in Him, "I shall not perish but have everlasting life." I clear my thought of all negation as I release the Law of the Living Spirit through my being. I reestablish the will to live as I embrace the exhilaration of vital and abundant Life. I know that He came "that I might have Life, and that I might have it more abundantly." I drink from the well of living water which bubbles up into everlasing Life. I live fully today by being alert to all that Life has to offer. I am a channel through which the mainstream of Life flows. I am Life in action. I express Life because I live. I live because He lives in me. I worship God in my reverence for all Life today. And so it is.

I Will Fear No Evil

<table>
<tr><td>**14**</td><td>**I FEAR NO EVIL**</td><td>Evil is merely the absence of good and is nothing in itself. Therefore it has no law governing its action. There is no evil in the Mind of God, only in the minds of men. What we believe to</td></tr>
</table>

be true becomes true for us. A belief in evil—disease, strife, limitation—activates the creative Law, and we experience the fruits of the bad seeds which we have planted. The forces of good are constantly at work among us, counteracting the evil tendencies of our ignorance; "but men loved darkness rather than light."

A little introspection will convince us that we are really afraid only of our own inadequacies and the doubts we have about our ability to cope with the situations of Life. Continued reasoning will show us that this is a completely groundless fear. It is true that we of ourselves can do nothing—until we put our Faith in God which strengthens us, and realize that "with God all things are possible."

Our job in Life is to enlist ourselves in the service of good and enlightenment by becoming disciples of the Lord. God is always on our side, and when we consciously put ourselves on His side, we have absolutely nothing to fear. The so-called power of evil is completely eliminated when we replace fear with Faith. Faith truly has the power to move mountains. What is there to be afraid of when we walk with the Lord, the great Law of Life—?

I fear no evil. Faith overcomes fear, and I believe only in good. God cannot desert me, even if He wanted to—which He doesn't. I glory in the good of Life today, I have conquered that which seemed evil and fearful yesterday. I see all problems as an opportunity to learn valuable lessons and to receive priceless experience. Everything unlike the nature of God is dissolved from my consciousness as I cleanse my subconscious of all fear, of all doubt, of all dread anticipation, and of all selfishness. I turn my mind inside out and take a good look at its contents. I put back only those thoughts, ideas, and attitudes which are clean, whole, constructive, and creative. This spiritual housecleaning sweeps out all evil, and I am filled with the beauty and goodness of the Presence and the Power of the Lord. And so it is.

For Thou Art with Me

15 **GOD IS WITHIN ME** Everything we are, do, say, think, and feel is an expression of God—of our concept of Him. We are God at the level of our expression. Think: "God is all of me. I am that part of Him which I can understand." That is why the Proverb instructs us, "Get wisdom: and with all thy getting get understanding." We must learn to really understand that what we are and experience indicates what we know of God. When we are unhappy with ourselves and what happens to us, the situation can only be remedied by learning more about the God which is within us. When we know Him more, we become more. There is no other way.

This God within is a living Reality. It seems that we still do not fully understand this principle. We believe it—to a point—but we need help with our unbelief. We are like the little girl who grasped her Sunday School teacher's explanation of God only sufficiently to report, "God is dead, and He is inside me." Think of God as Life. If It were not inside us, we would not live; since we live, It must be inside us. Let us thrill to this Inner Presence every moment, knowing that Its Will is to release Itself abundantly through us.

I cooperate with the free, full flow of Life through me today. I love Life and I live it abundantly. I know that God's Presence at the center of my being is His eternal gift and blessing to me and to all mankind. God exists. He exists in me. I exist in Him. He is constantly unfolding through me to produce increasingly more perfect patterns of Himself. I consciously cooperate with God today. I think in larger terms. The Law of Love is the Law of my life. I examine my life and refine its expression until it is a constant picture of God in action. What is true of God is true of me right now. I see God in all things and all people, and I live to express God so that all may see Him in me. I know I am His beloved, and I seek to please Him now. And so it is.

Thy Rod . . .

16 **SPIRIT IS MY ROD** The rod which supports and sustains us in every situation is the knowledge of the completeness of Spirit. Spirit is the One Whole Idea. It is the Word of God which was "in the beginning." The rod is the support upon which all knowledge and action is based. It is the active aspect of God. It is the One Mind, the Source of all Creation, the Absolute and Perfect First Cause. All experience and manifestation originate here. The rod is the Presence which is constantly with us. It is the Tree of Life, and everything else branches from it.

The rod is the main stream of Life. It is fluid and active at the same time that it is solid and strong. It is the symbol of Absolute Power. When the rod of the Spirit decrees a thing, it is already done. It is the sceptre which makes us rulers of our destiny when we wield it wisely, but it is also the means of punishing us when we depart from the Way of the Lord. The rod is our most priceless possession; without it we are nothing, but when we grasp it, it is the Divine Potential and the Infinite Possibility of the life of every individual.

The rod of Life is strong and flexible in my hands today. I am filled with vitality and strength. I know that I have in my hands the instrument of accomplishment. One Supreme Idea stands upright in my consciousness: I have complete awareness and Faith in the Absolute Power of the Lord. The rod of Spirit is the magic wand with which I transmute base material experience into the precious metal of accomplishment. I gain permanent possession of the rod by recognizing its power, grasping it firmly, and using it wisely. The rod is my prayer which I wave benevolently over all of Life's experience today. With the rod in my hand, I am the monarch of all I survey. I determine to execute my dominion wisely and benevolently. And so it is.

. . . *And Thy Staff* . . .

17 **MY STAFF IS THE LAW** The staff is the Law, which is the counterpart of the rod of Spirit. They are One, symbolizing the dual action of God as Spirit and Law, action and reaction, Presence and Principle, the personal and impersonal. The rod is the objective aspect of Infinite Mind which knows, while the staff is the subjective action which does. One is incomplete without the other, because for every impression there must be an expression. Involution automatically activates evolution. Every idea has within it the mechanics for expressing its own potential. When something is known, there is a natural Force which forms it into manifestation.

These two aspects of the One Mind are the basis of our teaching and the starting point for all spiritual understanding. The rod and the staff are the two pillars of the temple of individual consciousness, and both of them are necessary to support the arch of existence of which the Christ Individuality is the keystone. The rod and the staff guard the entrance to the Holy of Holies. We cannot enter in unless we utilize and cooperate with both the Spirit and the Law. They are One working two ways. Where does the function cease of either side of a pair of scissors?

I utilize my staff every step of the way. It clears the path before me and lifts me over the rocky places. It clears the tangled undergrowth from before me, and its great height assists me in vaulting over the swamps and marshes of despondent thought. This staff is my strength. It is always available for me to use. I can accomplish nothing without it, but I can accomplish anything with it. Obviously, it is meant for me to use, so I never try to walk without it. Without the staff in my hand, I am just a man; with it, I am God in man. I put my Faith in this staff of the Law of Love, and when I do, the Lord directs my steps. And so it is.

. . . *They Comfort Me*

18 **I AM COM-FORTED** The knowledge that the rod and the staff of Life are ours to use is a very comforting thought indeed, but as is true with any other of Life's tools, they can accomplish only what the person using them determines. Therefore it is squarely up to us. "My word . . . shall not return unto me void, but it shall accomplish that which I please, and it shall prosper in the thing whereto I sent it." We can consciously create circumstances, and it is our sacred obligation to do so. The experience which comes to us is the result of God acting through us. Our job in life is to constantly enlarge the channels for Spirit to flow through.

Many people object to the idea of "using God." The question might well be asked, "What else could we use?" God is Life, and a life which does not use its potential and expand its possibilities is a life wasted. God is the Source of all things, and these things are to be used. The comfort which knowledge and Faith in God give us does not come without its attendant responsibility. Comfort comes from knowing that when we do all that we can, God will do the rest. If we know *what* we want, God knows *how* to do it. Is there any greater comfort than being acquainted with this basic principle of Life?

*I am comforted in knowing that my knowledge
of the Lord establishes me in balanced relationship with all of Life. I am comforted in knowing
that in everything I do, He is with me. His rod
and his staff are my constant support, and His
loving concern looks after me in every situation,
if I first look after myself. I am comforted in
knowing that the Good Shepherd voluntarily
assumes the responsibility of looking after His
flock, of which I am a charter member. I will
always belong. I will never be cast into outer
darkness. I am comforted in knowing that there
is That within me which sees me through, even
though I may lose my own way. My comfort is
my Faith in God. And so it is.*

Thou Art with Me; Thy Rod and Thy Staff They Comfort Me

19 **THE WAY IS PREPARED** The great lesson of the Psalm is that we can never get lost or be hurt or troubled for any period of time if we follow the Way of the Lord. What is this Way other than the recognition of the balanced working of the Law of Cause and Effect? The Law is the Way which is prepared for us. It is this Way which Jesus explains to us by saying, "I go to prepare a place for you. And if I go and prepare a place for you, I will come again, and receive you unto myself; that where I am, there ye may be also. And whither I go ye know, and the way ye know." The Perfect Thought for man's evolution into eventual perfection is an Idea in the Mind of God. It therefore follows that this Idea must manifest, because that is the Law. Thought is demonstration in its invisible aspect. Manifestation is thought made visible. Both are real.

The evolution of thought into form can be compared to an arrow aimed straight and true, being released, and striking the bull's-eye of the target. At any stage of the process, the action seems incomplete unless we see the whole picture. When we see the relationship between all the parts of Creation, we understand the poet as he sings, "Trailing clouds of glory we come, from God who is our home." That is, we have been *thought* into existence by the Infinite Mind. The One Intelligence is incapable of creating anything imperfect, therefore we must be perfect. The path of evolution is the Way we travel on the journey toward discovering this Truth for ourselves.

Today I take another step on the journey to my long home. The Lord has prepared a beautiful Way for me to travel, and I have His company every step of the Way. I make the most of every moment in this wonderful Life. There is nothing too small to escape my attention. I know that "Trifles make perfection, and perfection is no trifle." There is nothing large enough to strain my imagination. I know that "with God, all things are possible." As I grow in wisdom and understanding, the Way opens before me. The spiritual compass of the Higher Self within keeps me on the Path. I love the Law which regulates my progress along the Way of Life. I give thanks for the part I play in my own destiny. I am happy to be a partner with God in this business of living. I do my best to fulfill my part of the bargain today and always. And so it is.

Thou Preparest a Table before Me . . .

20 **LIFE IS A FEAST**

At this point in the Psalm, we are told that a table is prepared for us. This is the place where the banquet is spread. All that we need for nourishment, accomplishment, and enjoyment are part of the substance of Life. These gifts are already given to us; we just need to attain them. What we earn we shall receive, and, as "the fields are white already unto the harvest," so the table is already prepared for the great occasion of the coming of the Lord. When we see Him as He is, we will recognize our right to sit with Him at the table of Life and to eat fully and drink deeply of all that it has to offer.

Upon this Cosmic Table are all the ingredients necessary to create, sustain, and maintain us. The wine represents the vitality of Spirit; the meat represents the strength and power of Spirit; the bread represents the substance of Spirit; the fish represents the productivity of Mind as Spirit; the fowl represents the freedom of Spirit; the vegetables represent the fertility of Spirit; the fruits represent the rewards of Spirit. What a repast has been prepared for us! Why should we hunger in the midst of such plenty? Only because we don't have Faith that it is really there. We forget that He has prepared a table for us and all we need to do is to help ourselves.

I drink deeply and eat fully of the Spirit and the Substance of Life today. I am a permanent guest in the house of the Lord. I give thanks for His warm and loving hospitality. I give thanks for the magnificence and luxury of the furnishings of His house. I hunger, and my appetite is sated by the taste and nourishment of the repast which is spread before me. I know that God is blessing every morsel of the food of thought, emotion, and experience in my life. I know that the many courses of the Feast of Life are to be shared equally by all. There is exactly the right food in sufficient quantities for all of us. I refrain from grasping or gorging because I know there is no end to supply. Another table is already spread in the next room, and another banquet is already being prepared in the kitchen of Life. And so it is.

. . . In the Presence of Mine Enemies

21 **I MAKE PEACE WITH MY ENEMIES** The only enemies we can possibly have are those of our own household. It is there that the Psalm tells us the Lord has prepared the feast for us. How forgiving and all-embracing is Divine Love! God loves us anyway, no matter what we have been, thought, or done. It is His great example of Love which gives us the power to rid ourselves of the corroding influence of negative and unworthy thoughts and attitudes. If we don't like the way we are, the only remedy is to simply stop being that way. When we want to change, we will find the way and the strength to change. Through prayer and right thinking and living, God is always available to help us make peace with ourselves. When the new broom sweeps clean, the old unpleasant personal traits go out the window, and we are "transformed by the renewing of our minds."

It has been said that a man is his own worst enemy. If this has any basis in fact, it must also follow that each of us is his own best friend—save one: God, the All-Good. "To have a friend, be a friend" is the rule to follow in clearing all enmity from our lives. The starting point is with the contents of our own minds and emotions. When we like what is there, we will be a friend to all, and all will be our friends. A mental equivalent of friendship will activate Love as the Law of our lives.

*I love Life, and I love the Lord as the Prince of
Peace within me. I eliminate all quarrelsome
and troublesome thoughts from my consciousness
today. I do not allow any enemies to reside in
the household of my mind. I am loving and
forgiving toward myself and toward all people.
All irritation and selfishness are removed from
my subconscious mind as I consciously "do unto
others as I would have others do unto me."
From the heaven of friendship within my heart,
I become friendly to my own inner being and a
friend to all the world. The rule of my life is the
new commandment which He has given unto us,
"that ye love one another." And so it is.*

Thou Anointest My Head with Oil

22 GOD KNOWS MY DIVINITY

We are what we are through the grace of God. It is the Father who anoints us, but it is through the Christ that we discover our own divinity. It is by a growing awareness of the Lord—the Law of Life—that we progress into Christ-Consciousness. Note that during the first part of the Psalm, the Lord—the Law—is spoken of in the formal third person as "He." But when the point of no return—the "valley of death"—is walked through, who is with us? "Thou art with me." The Inner Presence is now a Reality, and we address Him familiarly in the second person as "Thou."

This change in grammatical form is not by accident. It indicates a growing awareness of the Father within—the Christ. The Christ is the Divine Individuality of each of us. Awareness makes this Presence personal, and Love and Faith together are the Principle of the Christ in action which we know as the Lord—the Law. Metaphysically, "the Lord Christ" represents the two basic ingredients of all spiritual Truth: the Presence and the Principle, the Spirit and the Law.

The inner understanding of this mystical relationship is the "oil" with which we are anointed in this part of the Psalm. We are now royalty—the embodiment of enlightenment and power.

My mind is anointed with the oil of Spirit today. I understand the relationship between God and man, between Heaven and earth, between thought and thing, between cause and effect. I know that one with God is a majority. I know that as I think in my heart, so am I. I see the larger significance and purpose back of all experience. I recognize myself and all people as being parts of the One Great Whole. All knowledge and all power are available to me by the action of Spirit unfolding through Law. I am anointed, ordained, and Christened in the family of the Lord today. And so it is.

Thou Anointest My Head with Oil

23

I KNOW MY PURPOSE

It is the head which is anointed. The head represents the capacity to know. When we develop this capacity to the point where we can consciously perceive Spiritual Truth, anointment is automatic. We are initiated into the awareness of knowledge and the use of power when we evolve to the point of knowing that we are One with Spirit and Law. Anointment is a stage in our evolution and marks the ascendancy of Spirit in the human mind. Anointment precedes crucifixion, the next phase of spiritual initiation, which also takes place in the mind—"Golgotha, the sign of the skull"—when spiritual understanding crosses all limitation out of the individual consciousness.

We must consciously perceive and decide to follow the only possible purpose in individual human existence—to express God in all that we do. This is the key to Life's treasure chest. This is all we need to know and all there is to know—except how to do it. The "how" is revealed to us as we learn to ask the question "Does this express the true nature of God?" as the criterion of everything we think, say, or do. This standard is the symbol of anointment and eternally marks us as members of His legions.

I affirm my spiritual purpose in Life by living my awareness of God in every possible way. I never allow myself to lose sight of the Larger Picture. I keep constructive purpose constantly and clearly defined in my mind. I refuse to let myself be bogged down by trivialities; I focus attention upon being "about my Father's business." I never react TO anything in the outer but discipline myself to always act FROM the spiritual awareness of the Christ within. My purpose in life is to do the best possible job I can in being a whole person. This automatically accomplishes everything else. "I and the Father are One. He who hath seen me hath seen the Father." And so it is.

My Cup Runneth Over

24 **I AM SELF-EMPTIED AND GOD-FILLED**

"He who loses his life shall find it." We cannot experience the abundance of God until we have conquered the limitations of self. It is impossible to fill our cups to overflowing with the eternal riches of Spirit when their capacity is restricted by the sediment of worldly and materialistic concepts and habits.

The cup spoken of here in the Psalm indicates the individual consciousness. Up to this point the Psalm has instructed us in the steps of self-discipline and self-conquest which bring us through the various stages of blind Love and Faith in the Lord up to the conscious awareness of the Christ as the true Higher Self. This growing process of anointment serves to tip the cup so that everything undesirable in thought and attitude runs out. This requires constant personal discipline in meditation, prayer, treatment, and living. But as we empty ourselves daily, the Law automatically fills us with the vital flow of Spirit as we place our minds upon the reality and abundant attributes of Infinite Mind. "Nature abhors a vacuum," so when we take care of the denial of evil—the emptying process—Life takes care of the affirmation of Good—the filling process.

Let us remember that cups are designed to be used for the efficient and convenient handling of liquids. Metaphysically, fluids symbolize aspects of the Spirit. Let us not abuse our cups of consciousness by forcing them to hold base and inflexible solids. Thought must be kept free so that Spirit may flow. Use Life; don't abuse it.

I am a vessel of the Lord. The cup of my consciousness is forged from the raw stuff of Life, enlivened and enlightened by the pure essence of Spirit. My cup represents what I am, and I develop it into a constantly expanding and increasingly flexible receptacle of Good. I drink deeply from the cup of Life today. My cup represents the Infinite Capacity available for individual use. I experience expansion as I free my soul from the bondage of resentments, opinions, and prejudices. Forgiveness, open-mindedness, and Love are the precious metals which give my cup form as it is manifested into the Holy Grail of Spirit today. And so it is.

Surely Goodness and Mercy Shall Follow Me All the Days of My Life

25 **I EXPERI- ENCE GOD'S ABUNDANCE** It is impossible to conceive of a Loving Providence which could withhold Its Good from Its Creation. The feast is always prepared; the cup is always running over. Abundance and plenty are being manifested constantly throughout all of Creation. What, then, keeps us from seeing and experiencing this abundance? Just this: in the perfect functioning of Universal Law, abundance is determined by acceptance as well as by supply. Supply is Universal, maximum, and unvarying; acceptance is personal and therefore variable and often minimum. Supply is Being; acceptance is becoming. Supply is of God; acceptance is of man.

So we see that in any situation of lack, the problem is not one of supply but of distribution. Distribution is regulated by individual acceptance. Acceptance determines experience. A successful businessman uses as his credo "Think big and you'll be big." Countless numbers of people have found a new freedom and understanding of Life's real values through affirmative spiritual philosophies which teach that God is the Source of our supply— of all supply. "Praise God from Whom all blessings flow," and let us praise ourselves as the channels through which they pour.

God's Universe is one of complete and perfect
abundance. I am an individual expression of the
Universe. All the Laws which are true and active
in the Universe are true and active in me now.
It is true that God cannot express lack, because
there is no idea of lack in His mind. Therefore, I
can only experience abundance, because my mind
is the use I make of the One Mind. I build the
mental equivalent of plenty within my conscious-
ness today. I stop worrying about whether or not
there is enough to go around, because I know
there always is. Whatever I need I always have
at the instant I need it. God cannot withhold;
He can only give. I cannot reject; I can only
accept. "Father, I do give thanks for the
abundance which is mine." And so it is.

Surely Goodness and Mercy Shall Follow Me All the Days of My Life

26 **I AM A GOOD PERSON**

What more noble purpose and lofty ambition could one have in Life than to be a good person? What better guarantee can we have of becoming a good person than to impress upon our consciousness the ideal of goodness and then live according to this ideal? Complete goodness results from living by the Law. God alone is completely Good, and as we are created in His image and likeness, we are innately Good, and potentially Good—that is, like God.

The Psalm tells us that "goodness and mercy shall follow me all the days of my life." At this point in the Psalm, we have become One with the Lord. The three steps in the Psalm in which we have regarded the Lord are: third person—"He"—separateness; second person—"Thou"—togetherness; first person—"I"—Oneness. Of course, these three states of consciousness represent the three steps in demonstration: recognition, unification, and realization.

When spiritual values are uppermost in our minds and hearts, good works, good deeds, good health, good fortune, and good experience naturally follow. The movement is from within outward. The effect always follows the cause.

I find new and greater ways to do good today. I determine to so order and discipline myself that every thought reflects the purity of Spirit. I control my emotions so that my every response reflects peace and calm. I work so that my every deed and action may be taken as an example of behavior for all people. I seek to be good with the Goodness of God. Honesty of intention and purity of motive mold my life into a pattern of good. I find Life and I see only good in other people. I expect good, and good happens. I see only the good in everything and every situation. I have taste and use for only that which is good. I am becoming a good person now. And so it is.

Surely Goodness and Mercy Shall Follow Me All the Days of My Life

27 GOD IS ALWAYS MERCIFUL

Once upon a time a worn and tired traveler stopped at a farmer's cottage and asked for lodging for the night. In the moment of indecision before offering his hospitality, the farmer felt a great wave of love and kindness sweep over him and it was as if the voice of the Lord spoke, saying: "For I was an hungered, and ye gave me meat: I was thirsty, and ye gave me drink: I was a stranger, and ye took me in: naked, and ye clothed me: I was sick, and ye visited me: I was in prison, and ye came unto me." The farmer decided that he was being instructed to take the stranger in, and he did.

However, the farmer was disillusioned a short time later by the flatly atheistic statements of his guest, who mocked God and disclaimed all belief in any Higher Power. Outraged and unforgiving, the farmer threw the traveler out into the cold and darkness without even so much as a bite of supper. Somewhat proud of his "righteous indignation," the farmer bolted the door securely and was preparing for bed when the voice of the Lord gently reproached him asking, "Didn't I instruct you to care for the stranger?"

"Yes, Father, you did—and I intended to," the farmer replied, startled. "Then what happened?" the Lord questioned.

"That ungrateful person said that he didn't believe in you, Father, so I kicked him out," the farmer stated self-righteously.

"My son, let me tell you something," admonished the Lord; "I have put up with that man for over fifty years. Couldn't you stand him for just one night?"

I know that I am the recipient of mercy which has no restrictions. God continually and eternally showers His mercy upon all Creation. I am the recipient of His wonderful blessing of Love. Love is the essence of mercy. Compassion is mercy in action. Understanding is the result. I love and understand all people today, because I thrill to the knowledge that God loves and understands me. I have already received the benefit of the doubt from God in every aspect of my life. I make a sincere effort to temper all of my judgments with mercy. Mercy is my way of life as I remember His promise, "Inasmuch as ye have done it unto one of the least of these my brethren, ye have done it unto me." And so it is.

Surely Goodness and Mercy Shall Follow Me All the Days of My Life

28 **GOOD WORKS FOLLOW GOOD THOUGHT** Everyone has a deep inner desire to lead a good life, to do good works, and to enjoy good things. However, the good of life has a way of escaping us unless we understand the basic principle that we can only express and experience that good in the outer which we have first accepted and believed within ourselves. It is all a matter of Unity. As Emerson says, "To have a friend, be a friend." Also to have good, be good.

It is well to remember that "good" and "God" are basically the same word. God is the All-Good. The lesson at this point in the Psalm is that goodness and mercy follow when we identify ourselves intellectually and emotionally with these qualities. We are naturally one with them spiritually, because goodness and mercy are aspects of God, and our individual spiritual nature is God present within us. The Psalm brings us to this realization of Oneness at every level of consciousness, because what we are at the highest—or spiritual—level we must eventually become in all of our experience. It is really a matter of "Eventually; why not now?" Or, again, as Jesus says, "Seek ye first the kingdom of God, and His righteousness; and all these things shall be added unto you."

Today I start to work at the core of my being. I do my inner preparation before I attempt any outer activity. What I accept within, I experience in the outer. My prayer is the recipe for the beauty, goodness, and abundance of the life which I lead. I expect to be healed because I am willing to change my character and personality so that healing is possible through me. I expect to experience love and understanding to the degree that I express love and understanding toward others. As I rid myself of selfishness and irritation, I expect to experience abundance and happiness. I give up all false belief that I can get something for nothing. I pay my way in coin of the spiritual realm—Good, Truth, Beauty. I plant wisely today. I know that good seed produces a good harvest. And so it is.

Surely Goodness and Mercy Shall Follow Me All the Days of My Life

29 **EACH DAY IS BLESSED** One day has the same potential as any other day—unlimited possibility and unrestricted opportunity. God created us in His image and likeness and has left us alone to discover this fact for ourselves. To make this discovery, we must keep eternally at it, because we attain this realization by degrees. The days of our lives represent these degrees of awakening and understanding.

In the Bible, the "day" represents light and understanding, while the "night" symbolizes darkness and ignorance. This gives the Psalm a much deeper meaning than does the idea of the conventional "day" as a unit of twenty-four hours in time. As the Psalmist states "Surely goodness and mercy shall follow me all the days of my life," he is drawing a conclusion from the evidence which has been amassed during the previous spiritual reasoning of the Psalm toward God-realization. When this sense of Unity is achieved, *surely* goodness and mercy must follow. The "days of my life" are our points of awareness of spiritual Truth. When a point of spiritual Truth becomes clear in our minds, all good things take place in our lives. God is blessing each day according to our individual understanding.

God has given me this day. I determine to make the best possible use of it. I know that "now am I a son of God and it does not yet appear what I shall be." There are unlimited opportunities to grow and to do good today and every day. God has created me free from limitation, and I impose none. God is blessing my day. God indwells my every thought and action. I forget yesterday and I do not worry about tomorrow. I have plenty to think about and do today. I can live a lifetime in a moment. I can glimpse eternity in an instant. I free myself from all bondage of time. I have all the time there is. I live in God's time as my day of knowing extends through all eternity. Father, I do give thanks for this day and the fullness thereof. And so it is.

And I Will Dwell in the House of the Lord Forever

<table>
<tr><td>

30

</td><td>

**HEAVEN
IS MY
HABITATION**

</td><td>

*"Neither shall they say, Lo here! or, lo there!
for, behold, the kingdom of God is within you."*

</td></tr>
</table>

Thus, Jesus gives us the key to the inner mystery of Life. It is further clarified with the sample phrase, "Our Father, which art in heaven," and when the Psalmist says, "If I ascend up into heaven, thou art there: if I make my bed in hell, behold, thou art there," we begin to grasp the fact that we are in heaven right now. All we have to do is to accept it.

Heaven is our natural dwelling-place. It is truly the "house of the Lord." Any time we are not in heaven, we are away from home. When this happens, our job is to stop "wandering in a far country" and get back into our Father's House. Heaven happens as the result of our care and persistence in seeing that it can happen in our own hearts. Heaven is the state of balanced consciousness. Constructive thinking and controlled feeling order and maintain this balance. The materials are always available for us to build our house in heaven. A practical spiritual approach to Life, a love for God and all people, an honest desire to serve, and an abiding Faith, are all consistently necessary in order to attain residence in the Kingdom of Heaven.

I am in heaven today. I dwell here forever. I will take no more trips into the lower regions of fear, despondency, and despair. I live in faith, expectancy, and joy. I see heaven all around me. My vision is clear and I see all things rightly. When I "judge not according to the appearance, but judge righteous judgment," this world becomes for me the Kingdom of Heaven. I know that my world is the product of my inner consciousness. I maintain my inner life at the heaven level, and my world corresponds accordingly. I stop trying to take the gates of heaven by storm. I realize that I already dwell there. I affirm my unity with Infinite Mind, and heaven is the result. I follow the Way of Heaven in all that I do. I am in the Kingdom of Heaven and it is within me, and "I will dwell in the house of the Lord forever." And so it is.

And I Will Dwell in the House of the Lord Forever

31 **I LIVE FOREVER** That which lives can never die. Life is continuous, without beginning or end, ever evolving into greater, more perfect patterns of expression. Life is the movement of Spirit and the action of Love. We have been entrusted with the gift of Life and have been left free to do with it what we will. What we fail to realize, sometimes, is that no matter what we do with it, Life persists and continues to express Itself, although sometimes it is severely hampered by our lack of cooperation.

In times of trouble or discouragement, it is a great help to say, "Wake up and live!" We have to solve our problems sometime. We cannot avoid or evade our spiritual responsibility as a living action of God. Anything glossed over or left undone will only turn up in our lives again. Jesus said, "I am come that they might have Life, and that they might have it more abundantly." This is our heritage, our challenge, and our responsibility. Let us recognize it and live accordingly.

There is no terminal point to Life. What we are living in this earthly life is merely one phase of our Larger Life. Death is an impossibility. Jesus dissolved it for all time by demonstrating Eternal Life and inviting us to follow in His path, saying, "Let not your heart be troubled: ye believe in God, believe also in me. In my Father's house are many mansions: if it were not so, I would have told you. I go to prepare a place for you. And if I go and prepare a place for you, I will come again, and receive you unto myself; that where I am, there ye may be also."

I am alive in the vast expanse of Eternity. I embrace Life, and I live it to the hilt. I have an irresistible will to live. All negative thoughts are dissolved from my mind. They have no place in the Abundant Life. All destructive emotions are replaced with attitudes of Love and Life. All harmful habits and activities are corrected to conform to the constructive Life urge and principle within me. I am attuned and receptive to the great blessing of Life today. As I experience Life, I am experiencing the continual presence and blessing of Divine Spirit and Infinite Law in every part of my life. "There is One Life. This Life is God. This Life is perfect. This Life is my life now"—and forever. And so it is.